What We Have in Common

A Brim Coloring Book

Written by Jane Landey
Edited by David Austin
Drawings by David Austin and Jane Austin

Copyright©2017

Printed in U.S.A.

No parts of the book should be transmitted or reproduced.

Introduction

What We Have in Common Brim Coloring Books enable children to color the drawings as they read along! The books display the similarities of related animals. In this series, the leopard and the cheetah are compared. The facts enable children to appreciate common values. Thus, imbibing in them an interest towards animals which could help them to appreciate what they have in common with one another.

The Leopard

And

The Cheetah

The leopard and the cheetah have things in common. They are animals with long bodies. They have spots on their bodies. Both are wild animals.

A leopard and a cheetah meet in a forest.

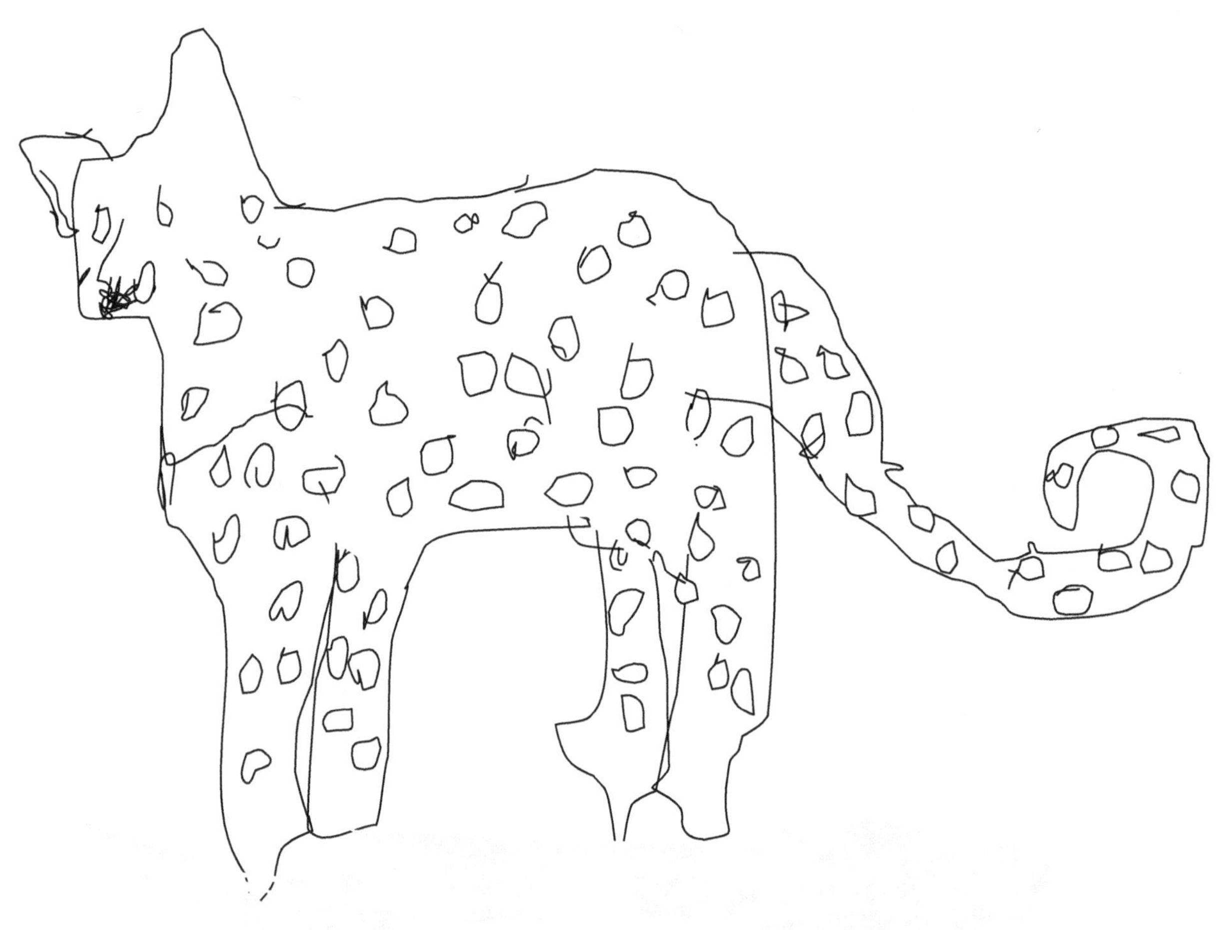

I am a leopard.

I am a cheetah.

I live in the forest.

I live in the forest too!

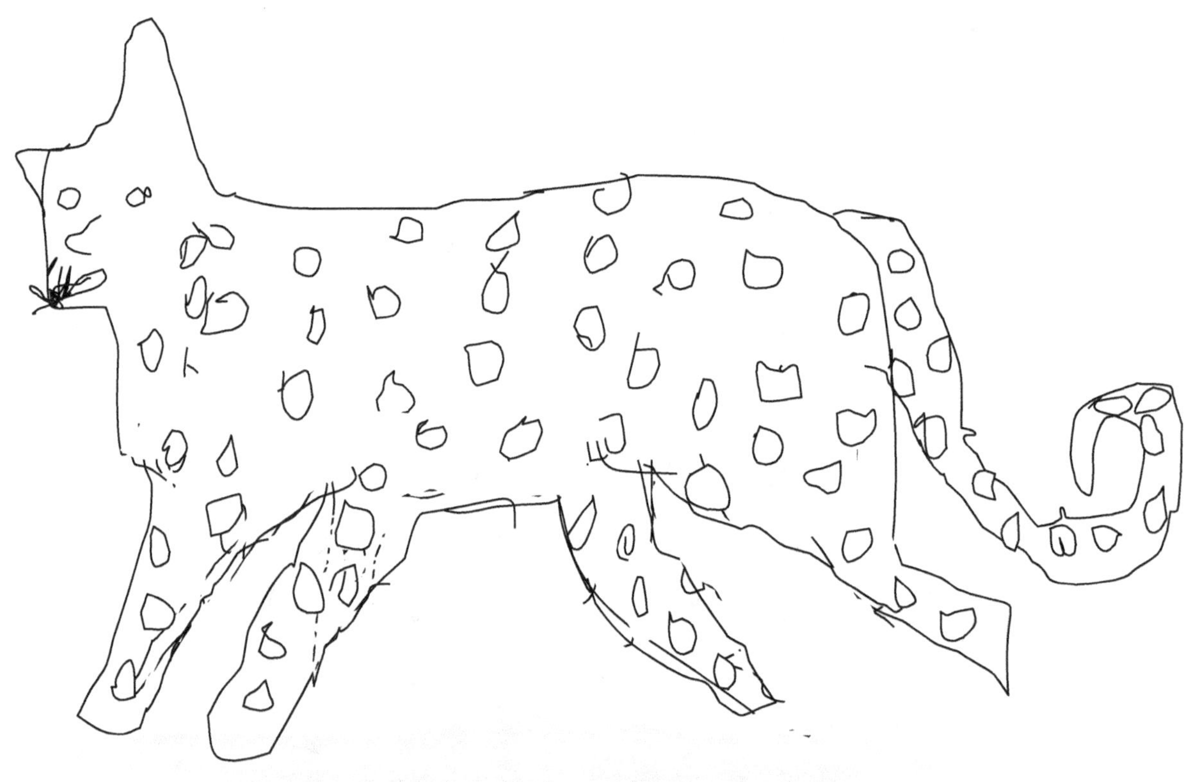

I can run very fast!

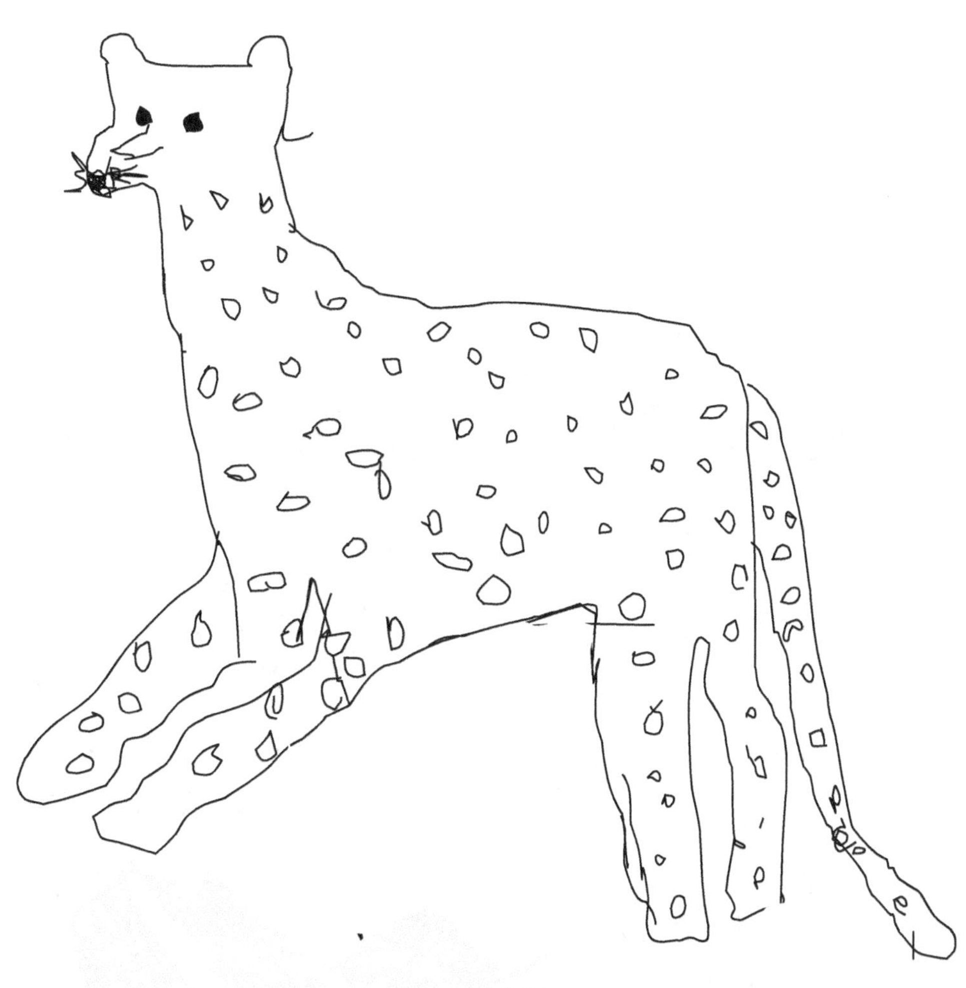

And I can run very fast too!

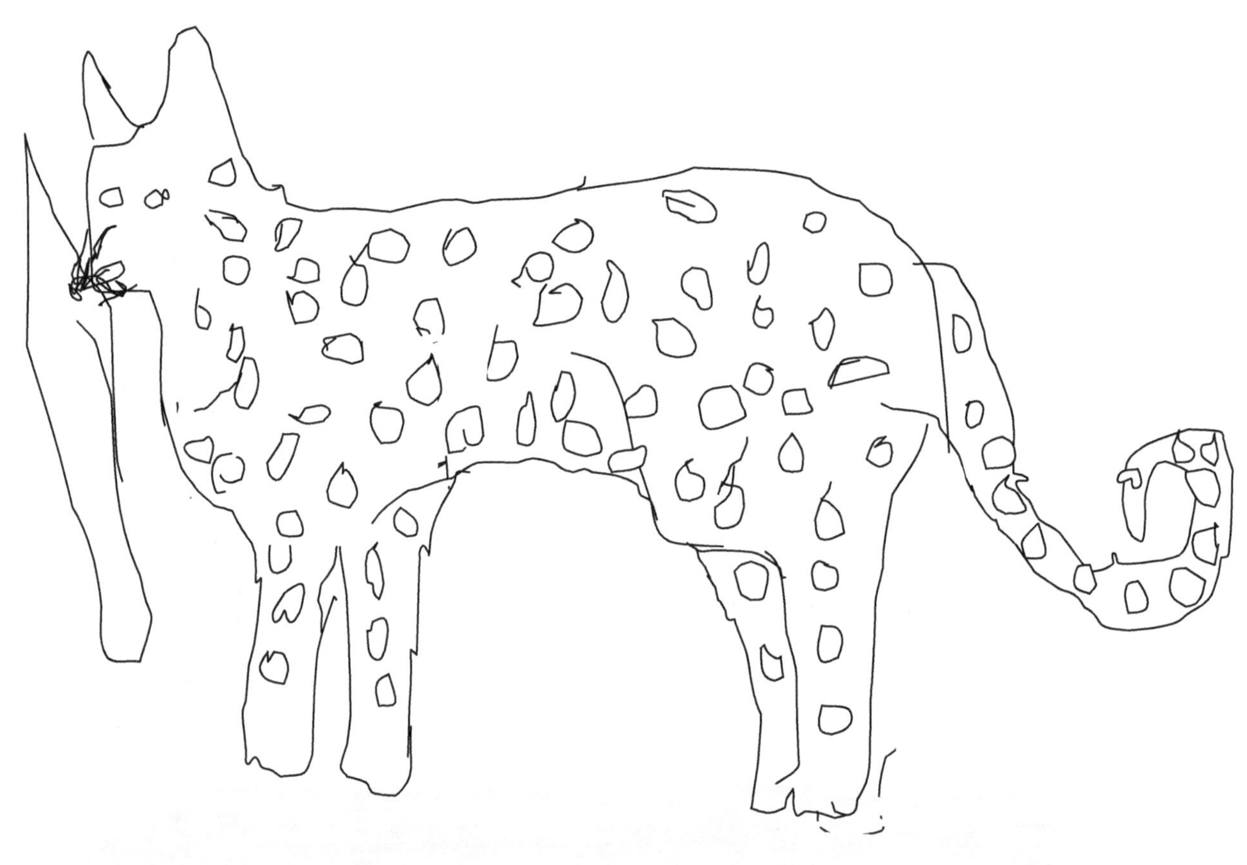

I love to eat raw meat.

And I love to eat raw meat too!

I can hide to catch an animal.

And I can hide to catch animal too!

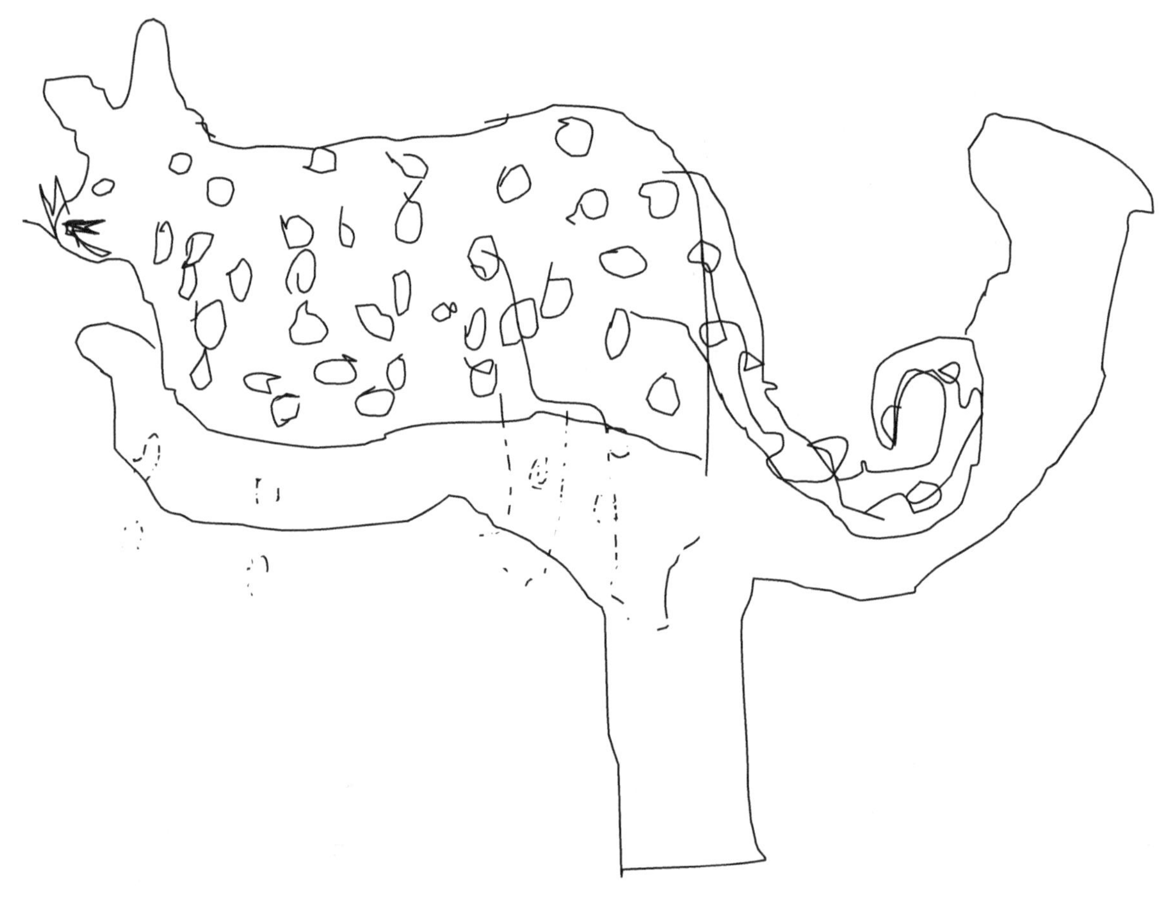

I can lie on a branch of a tree.

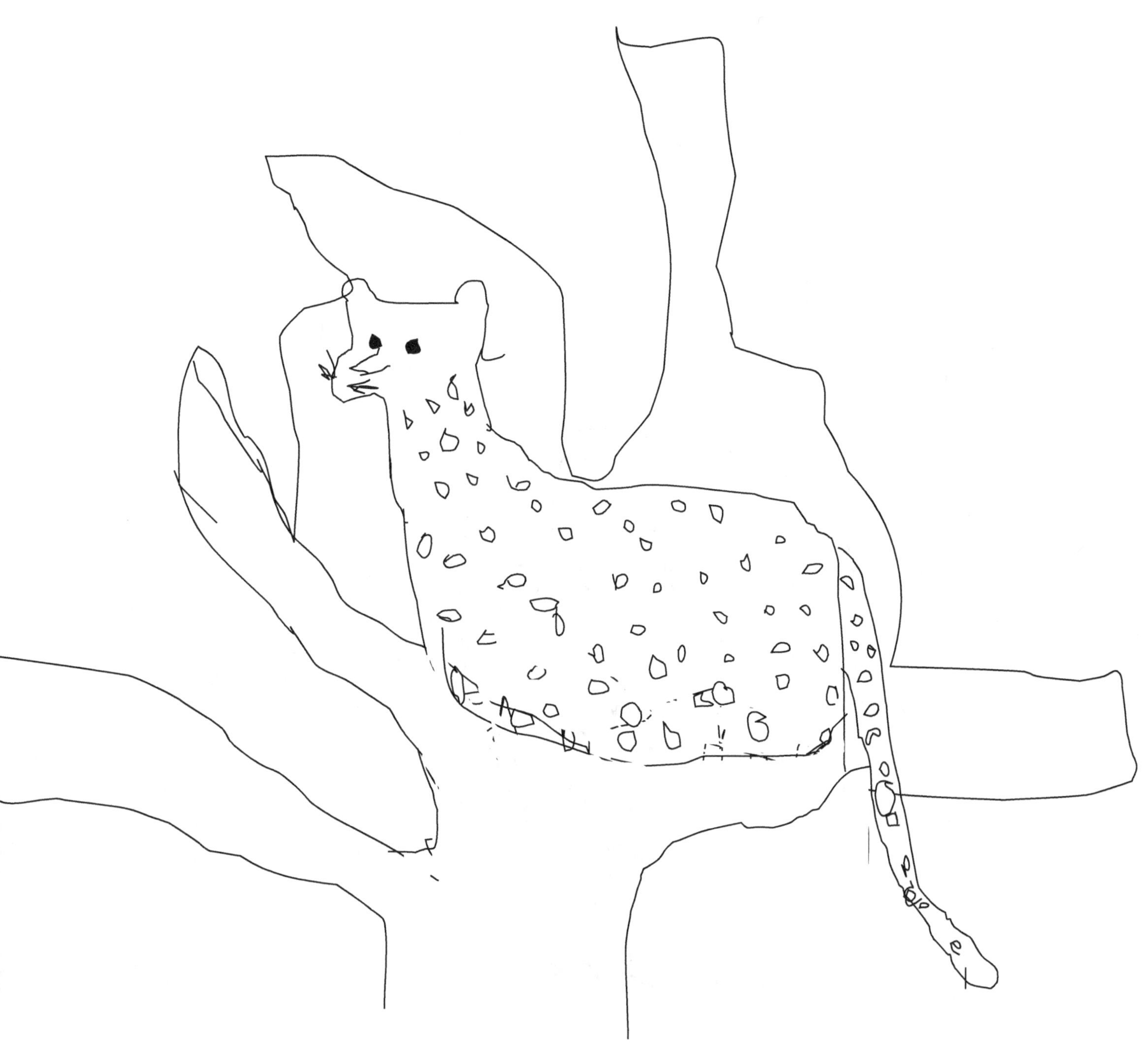

I can lie on a branch of a tree too!

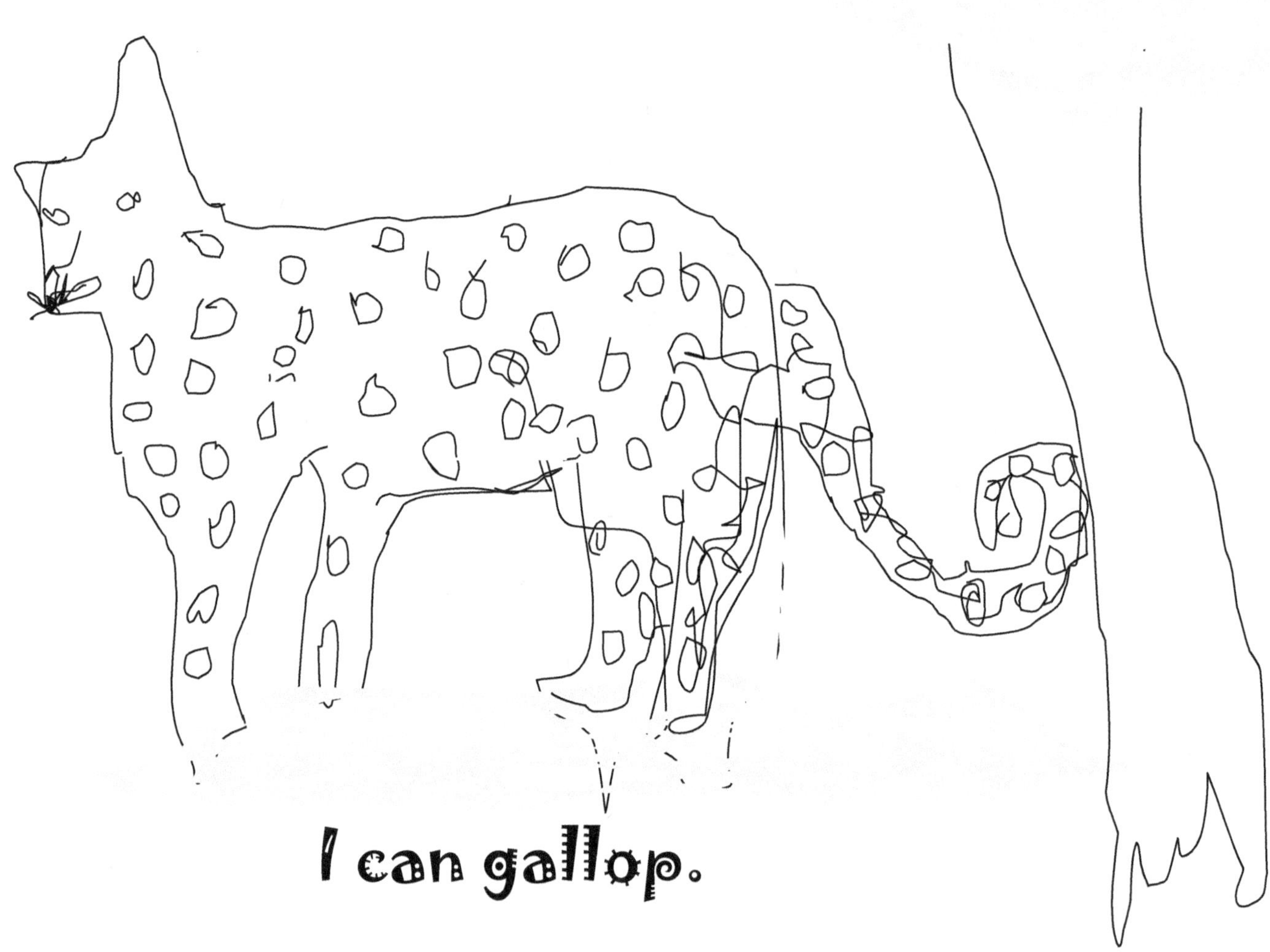

I can gallop.

I can gallop too!

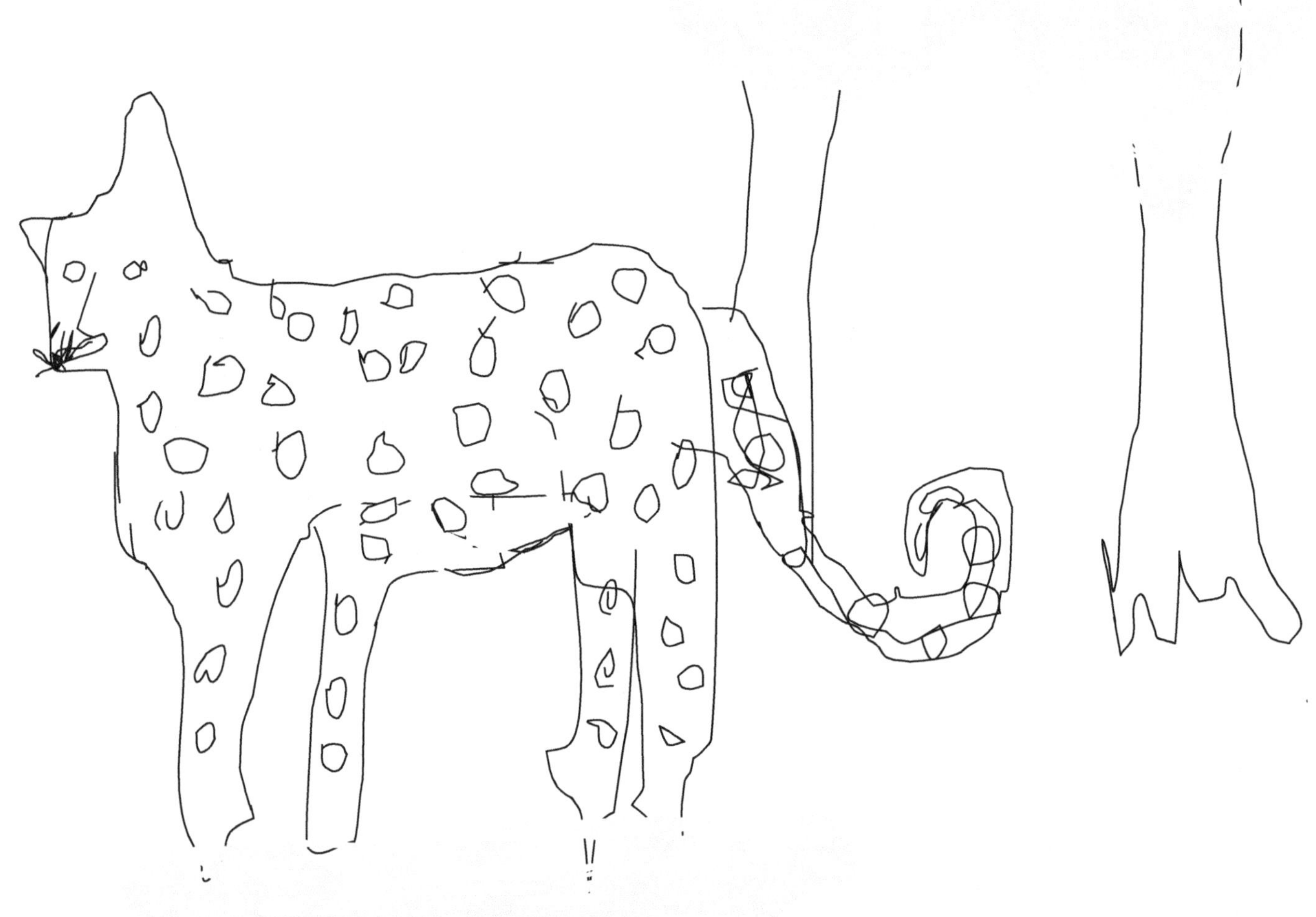

I smell animals from far away.

So do I!

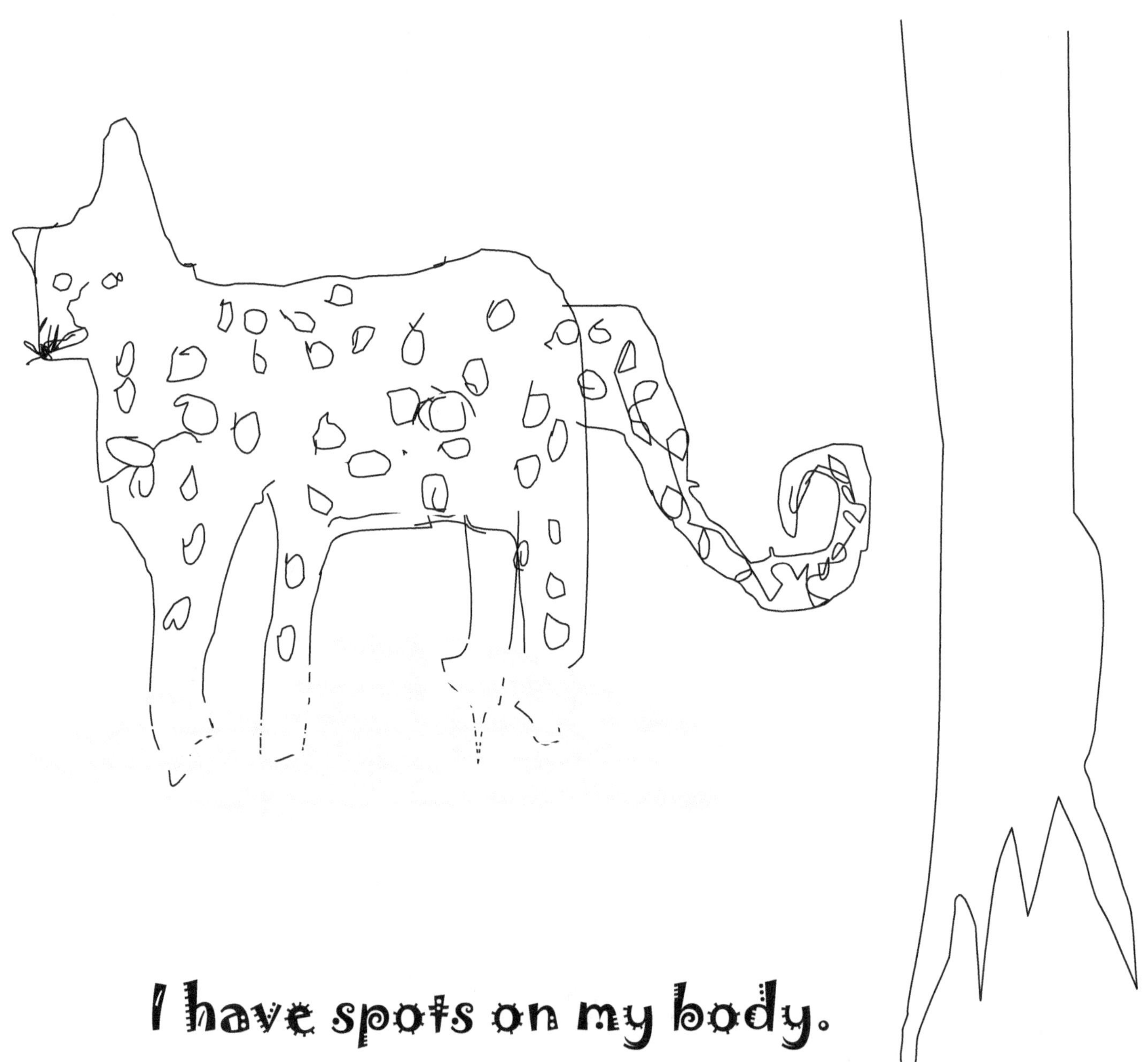

I have spots on my body.

I have spots on my body too!

My fur is yellow and it has big black spots.

My skin is yellow and it has small
black spots too!

My two ears hear sounds from far away.

My two ears hear sounds from far
away too!

I have a long tail.

I have a long tail too!

I have whiskers.

I have whiskers too!

My two eyes see clearly from far
away.

My two eyes see clearly from far away too just like you!

My four legs are strong.

My four legs are strong too!

I am going to look for an animal. I am hungry!

I am hungry too! I am going to look
for an animal myself!

What We Have in Common Brim Coloring Books

Crocodile and Alligator
Turtle and Tortoise
Starfish and Octopus
Worm and Snake
Turkey and Vulture
Ostrich and Emu
Weka and Kiwi
Bat and Rat
Camel and Llama
Duck and Pelican
Kangaroo and Wallaby
Pig and Tapir
Skunk and Squirrel
Hedge and Anteater
Cat and Owl
Elephant and Rhinoceros
Dog and fox
Buffalo and Bull
Leopard and Cheetah
Horse and Zebra